BEHIND THE SCENES

FLYING *THE* ATLANTIC

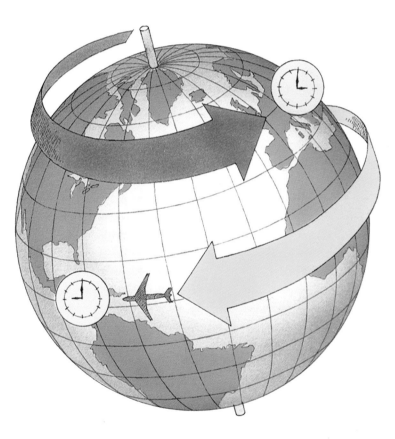

Written by Peter Mellett

Illustrated by Bill Donohoe

Heinemann
LIBRARY

First published in Great Britain by Heinemann Library, Halley Court,
Jordan Hill, Oxford OX2 8EJ, a division of Reed Educational and
Professional Publishing Ltd. Heinemann is a registered trademark of Reed
Educational & Professional Publishing Limited.

OXFORD MELBOURNE AUCKLAND BLANTYRE
IBADAN JOHANNESBURG GABORONE
PORTSMOUTH NH (USA) CHICAGO

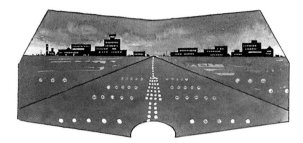

Editors: Alyson Jones, Andrew Farrow
Designer: John Kelly
Art Director: Joanna Hinton-Malivoire

Printed in Hong Kong

03 02 01 00 99
10 9 8 7 6 5 4 3 2 1

British Library Cataloguing in Publication Data
Mellett, Peter
Flying the Atlantic. - (Behind the scenes)
1.Air travel - Atlantic Ocean - Juvenile literature
I.Title
387.7'09163

ISBN 0 431 02162 7

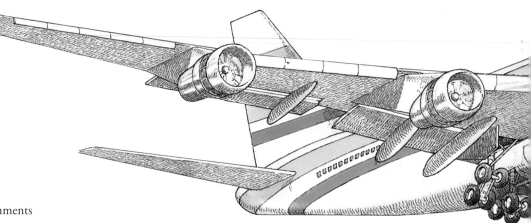

Acknowledgements
Our thanks to Captain Frank Bond for his comments
in the preparation of this book.

Every effort has been made to contact copyright holders of any
material reproduced in this book. Any omissions will be rectified in
subsequent printings if notice is given to the Publisher.

Any words appearing in the text in bold, **like this**, are explained in
the Glossary.

CONTENTS

4

WHO IS FLYING THE ATLANTIC?

Today is the start of your holiday in the USA. But first you must fly almost 5,000 kilometres across the Atlantic Ocean. Your tickets were booked weeks ago. You have packed all your suitcases and at last it is time to go. There are all sorts of things, like the plane, pilot, food, fuel and cabin staff, that need to come together to make your journey possible.

YOUR VERY OWN PLANE

At the moment the plane you will travel on is flying 10,000 metres high over Germany. It is flying towards the airport at 1,000 kph – ten times faster than a speeding car. Your plane is full of passengers travelling from Europe to the UK. Passenger aircraft average about 14 hours flying each day for their working lives.

PLENTY OF FUEL

Planes burn aviation fuel in their engines. This fuel is rather like the diesel oil used by lorries and buses. It is made at an oil refinery from crude oil. Road tankers bring the fuel to the airport where it is stored in huge tanks.

06.30 get up; get washed and dressed * 07.00 eat breakfast

07.45 taxi arrives; say your goodbyes; load all the luggage into the taxi

THE LITTLE THINGS YOU NEED

It is easy to forget about all the little things that will help to make your flight safe and pleasant. Stacked ready in the central stores there are mountains of cans, bottles and plastic cups.

There are also scented paper wipes, soap and towels, blankets and magazines. There are thousands of different items that must be provided clean, fresh and new for the start of every flight.

10.00 arrive at the airport (passengers should be there 2 hours before a flight is due to take off)

08.00 leave home * 08.45 stuck in a traffic jam on the motorway

YOUR ROUTE

Your flight will take you high above rain, snow and most storms. Bad weather can cause problems during a flight. The weather is fine at home, but an unusual storm is building up in the middle of the Atlantic Ocean. This storm may affect your flight during the hours to come.

WHAT YOU WILL EAT

You will have lunch on board the plane. Your food is one of 30,000 meals prepared yesterday in the airport kitchens. You only eat vegetarian food so you sent in a special order two weeks ago. The food is cooked and packed into these individual portions and then it is refrigerated.

CHECKING IN

You cannot climb aboard the plane as soon as you arrive at the airport. There are thousands of other passengers passing through the main **terminal building** and it will take about two hours for you to board your plane.
During this time you will meet some of the airport staff who look after you. But most of the staff work behind the scenes, helping to make sure the start of your journey runs smoothly.

CHECK-IN DESK

First you must find your airline's check-in desk. The passenger agent checks the flight tickets and hands each person a small printed card called a boarding card. She weighs your luggage and puts a sticker on each case.

HOW BIG?

Airports are enormous. The runways are up to 3 km long. The main terminal building holds about 1,000 staff and up to 15,000 passengers. Around the airport are service areas where fuel and cargo wait to be loaded on and off the planes.

10.15 queue for check-in desk.
Who's got the tickets – Mum or Dad?

ground control tower

check-in desks

baggage handlers

departure lounge

immigration

cafes/duty free

baggage reclaim

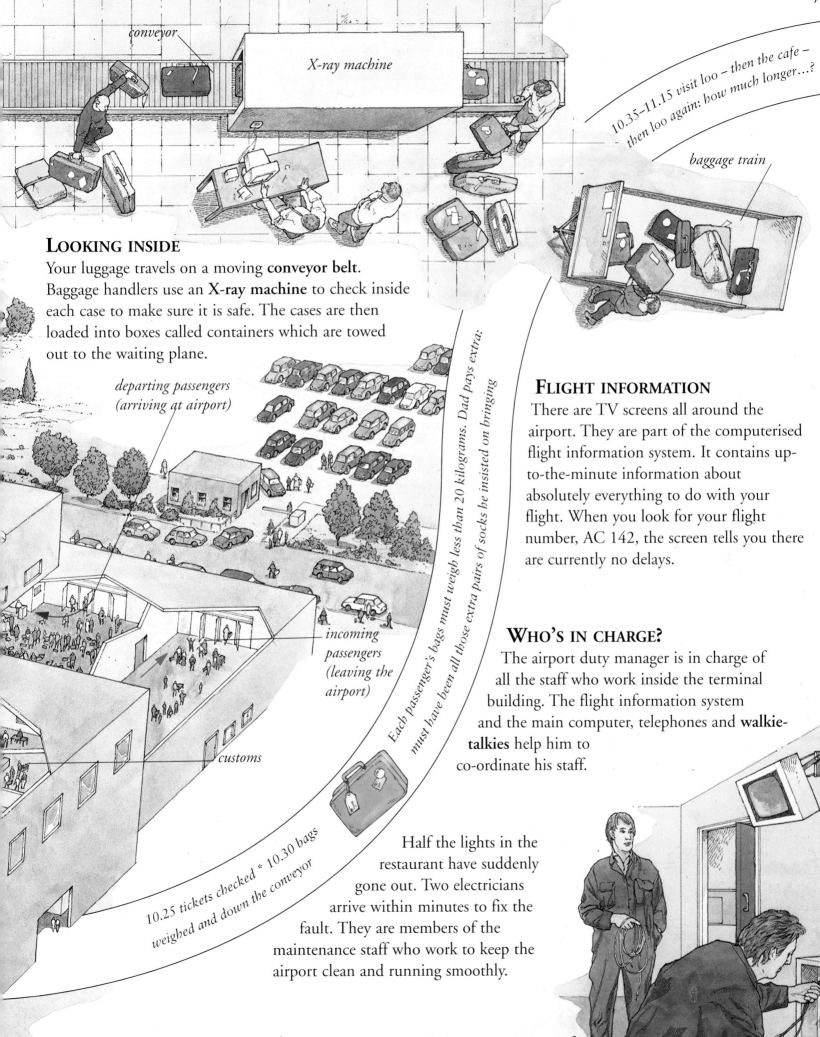

conveyor

X-ray machine

baggage train

10.35–11.15 visit loo – then the cafe – then loo again: how much longer…?

LOOKING INSIDE

Your luggage travels on a moving **conveyor belt**.
Baggage handlers use an **X-ray machine** to check inside
each case to make sure it is safe. The cases are then
loaded into boxes called containers which are towed
out to the waiting plane.

*departing passengers
(arriving at airport)*

Each passenger's bags must weigh less than 20 kilograms. Dad pays extra: must have been all those extra pairs of socks he insisted on bringing

FLIGHT INFORMATION

There are TV screens all around the
airport. They are part of the computerised
flight information system. It contains up-
to-the-minute information about
absolutely everything to do with your
flight. When you look for your flight
number, AC 142, the screen tells you there
are currently no delays.

*incoming
passengers
(leaving the
airport)*

WHO'S IN CHARGE?

The airport duty manager is in charge of
all the staff who work inside the terminal
building. The flight information system
and the main computer, telephones and **walkie-
talkies** help him to
co-ordinate his staff.

customs

*10.25 tickets checked * 10.30 bags weighed and down the conveyor*

Half the lights in the
restaurant have suddenly
gone out. Two electricians
arrive within minutes to fix the
fault. They are members of the
maintenance staff who work to keep the
airport clean and running smoothly.

TURNROUND

Here is the plane you're going to travel on – but it's not ready for you just yet. It arrived at the airport less than an hour ago, carrying 400 passengers. During their three-hour flight, each one of those passengers has eaten a meal, had some drinks, snoozed under a blanket and visited the toilet. There is a lot of clearing up and restocking to be done before you can go to your seat.

While you've been checking in and waiting, what has been happening to your plane?

Scented finger wipes

Butter

Bread roll

Salt and pepper

Plastic cutlery

Sugar

It can carry 420 passengers for 13,000 kilometres in a single flight – a third of the way round the world

IN-FLIGHT EATING

The food you'll eat during your flight will be an individual portion served on a tray. It is wheeled onto the plane inside refrigerated trolleys. What will your vegetarian meal be like?

HONEY WAGONS

During the last flight, more than 1,000 litres of dirty water and waste from the toilets and wash basins have been collected in tanks. This waste is pumped away in mobile tankers known as **honey wagons**.

RESTOCKING

Cleaners clear away piles of empty cups and drinks bottles, then sweep the floors and tidy the seats. They have to restock the plane with over 3,000 new items, including blankets, magazines and drinks.

Every day over 90,000 pieces of airline cutlery are washed in the airport's kitchens

ENGINEER'S INSPECTION

Engineers check that the plane is safe to fly. They inspect the outside for any obvious faults, and also the tyres, electrical circuits and oxygen supplies. If repairs are needed the engineer will 'ground' the plane and your flight will be delayed.

TWELVE ELEPHANTS

Luggage is carried underneath the passenger cabin in a space called the baggage hold. The baggage handlers have 23 tonnes of luggage to unload – that's the weight of 12 large elephants!

At last your plane is ready – is your flight being called over the public address system?

PILOT'S BRIEFING

In the briefing room, the captain and co-pilot decide which route to follow. Weather forecasts help them calculate how much fuel to take. More fuel is needed when the plane flies against strong winds.

It takes about 90 minutes to turn around your plane.
* About 400 planes take off or land each day

Engineers make over 200 pre-flight checks to your plane

a litre of fuel

FUEL

Fuel is pumped into the plane from underground pipes They unload up to 100,000 litres of fuel in about 20 minutes. In one hour the plane's engines burn 8,000 litres of aviation fuel – that's enough to run a family car for over six years. Our plane can go about 70 metres on a litre of fuel – a family car could go 150 times that far!

70 m

SECURITY ALERT

The open doorway you have just walked through is the **metal detector** machine. It searches each passenger for guns, knives or any other metal object they should not have. Pulses of electricity flow through coils of wire around the doorway. The coils create a magnetic field. Any metal object in the doorway sends back a tiny magnetic echo that sets off the alarm.

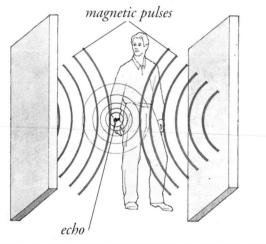

magnetic pulses

echo

*11.15 go through security checks * 11.30 enter departure area: visit the duty free shops*

DEPARTURES

You hear over the public address system: '*Passengers for flight AC 142 please pass into the departure area*'. You must now pass from the public part of the **terminal building**, through the security checks and into the departure area. Only people with tickets for the flight are allowed through.

PASSPORT CONTROL

You must show the officer at **passport control** three things: your **passport**, the boarding card and your ticket. The passport is issued by the government and shows your photograph and name. The boarding card gives your flight and seat number. It proves that earlier you checked in properly.

WHAT'S IN THE BAG?

Hand luggage is checked by an **X-ray machine**. X-rays are very powerful sorts of radio waves. They pass through the luggage and into a special camera linked to a TV screen. Solid objects absorb X-rays so they show up as shadowy silhouettes on the screen. If anything suspicious is seen, then the bag is opened and inspected more closely.

An x-ray image of a passenger's hand luggage.

*11.40 boarding call * 11.50 can't find Gate 12! Quick! Ask a security man * 12.05 walk on board*

AIRPORT COMMUNICATIONS

Many airport staff carry a **walkie-talkie** radio. Staff use them like cordless telephones to communicate with each other or receive instructions from managers. They can also talk to each other when they are trying to find any passengers who have not heard the boarding call.

Each group of staff has its own channel, or frequency so that they receive the right information. There was no need to tell the baggage handlers that the lights went out earlier in the restaurant!

ALL ABOARD

'Atlantic Carriers announce the departure of flight AC 142 to New York. Boarding now at Gate 12.' You follow the signs from the departure lounge and enter Gate 12. Inside the passageway you do not realise you are now outside the terminal building and 5 metres above the ground. At the end is the main passenger door of your plane. Welcome aboard!

READY FOR TAKE OFF

At last you are guided to your seat and are now waiting for take off. On the **flight deck**, the captain and co-pilot are busy working through about 100 items on a checklist. They look at the instruments and check lights and switches to make sure each part of the aircraft's machinery is working properly…

'*Starting systems?*' … '*On and checked*'.

PUSH BACK

'*Hello Ground Control – AC flight 142, stand C5 – permission to **push back?**'*
Your plane is parked with its nose facing the terminal building. A powerful vehicle called an **air tug** tows the plane from the **stand** onto the **taxiway** which leads to the runway. The air tug has large, wide tyres and low gearing to help it move the heavy plane.

TOTALLY DEPENDENT

The elevated walkway swings away from the plane. Lights blink on the captain's control panel to tell him the main doors are all shut. The plane is now airtight and sealed off from the outside world. You and more than 400 other people now depend entirely on the machinery inside the plane and the provisions it carries.

12.10 push back * 12.15 start to taxi * the wings look rather droopy. It must be all that fuel in the wing tanks

Red light at X *way*; two other planes cross your path

HELLO CONTROL TOWER...

The captain must always be in touch with controllers on the ground. 'Hello Control Tower – this is AC flight 142'... 'Hello AC 142 – this is Ground Control – you are cleared to **taxi** along A9 to 25R'... From the start to the finish of your flight – nearly 5,000 kilometres – someone somewhere will be watching you.

*Sharp turn left: all stop * 12.30 start of take off; why has Dad got his eyes shut?*

THRUST FORWARD

At the front of each jet engine are huge spinning fans called compressors. They draw in air that is squeezed and compressed by turbines inside the engine. Fuel burns in the compressed air to produce a roaring jet of super-hot exhaust gases. This jet provides the **thrust** that pushes the plane along: imagine 50 elephants sitting on your head – that's how much force is thrusting your plane forward when you take off.

TRAFFIC JAMS

It can take up to fifteen minutes to reach the start of the runway. Your plane is just one in a slowly-moving queue. Green lights down the middle of the taxiway mean 'carry on'. Red bars mean 'stop!'. The Ground Controller watches a **radar** screen in the control tower. The screen shows all the planes that are moving on the ground.

From the captain's point of view, taxiing is rather like driving a three-storey block of flats down a motorway

CLEARED FOR TAKE OFF

The pilot stops at the beginning of the runway. 'Hello AC 142 – this is Tower Control – you are cleared for take off'. The engine noise rises but the plane does not move. Suddenly the brakes are released. The thrust of the engines pushes you back into your seat and the plane starts to hurtle down the runway.

TAKING OFF

It takes the plane just 50 seconds to take off. In that time it reaches the same speed as a racing car – 380 tonnes of weight travelling at 300 kph! The engines are roaring at maximum **thrust** and the wheels rumble under you on the runway. Suddenly you feel as if you are hanging in mid-air at the top of a fairground roller coaster. The rumbling of the wheels stops. You are now airborne!

AIRFLOW

Aeroplane wings are called **aerofoils**. The top surface is curved and the underneath is flatter. The front of the wing slices the air into two streams. Air flowing over the top of a wing is stretched out, because it has to travel faster to meet up again with the air flowing under the wing.

lower pressure

upthrust on wing

air flow

wing

higher pressure

Air pressure above the wing is less than air pressure pushing upwards beneath the wing. The result is an upwards force called **lift**.

THE THREE STAGES OF TAKE OFF

There are three stages of take off – velocity-one (V1), velocity of rotation (Vr) and initial climb. V1 is the last moment the pilot can decide to abort the take off and stop. Vr is the speed at which the plane lifts off. When the plane is travelling a bit faster than Vr, the pilot lifts the nose and the plane starts to climb.

GETTING STREAMLINED

As soon as possible after take off, the captain raises the **undercarriage** wheels into the plane's wings and belly.

Planes have a sleek **streamlined** shape so that they slice smoothly through the air. Air cannot flow easily around the lumpy shapes of the wheels. They produce a force called **drag** which holds the plane back.

12.31 take off * 12.40 air traffic controllers on the ground order a change of course – they have spotted a flock of migrating geese on the radar

12.45 cabin staff check the stores on the plane – have they got your dinner?

12.55 cruising height of 10,000 metres – about 10 kilometres high

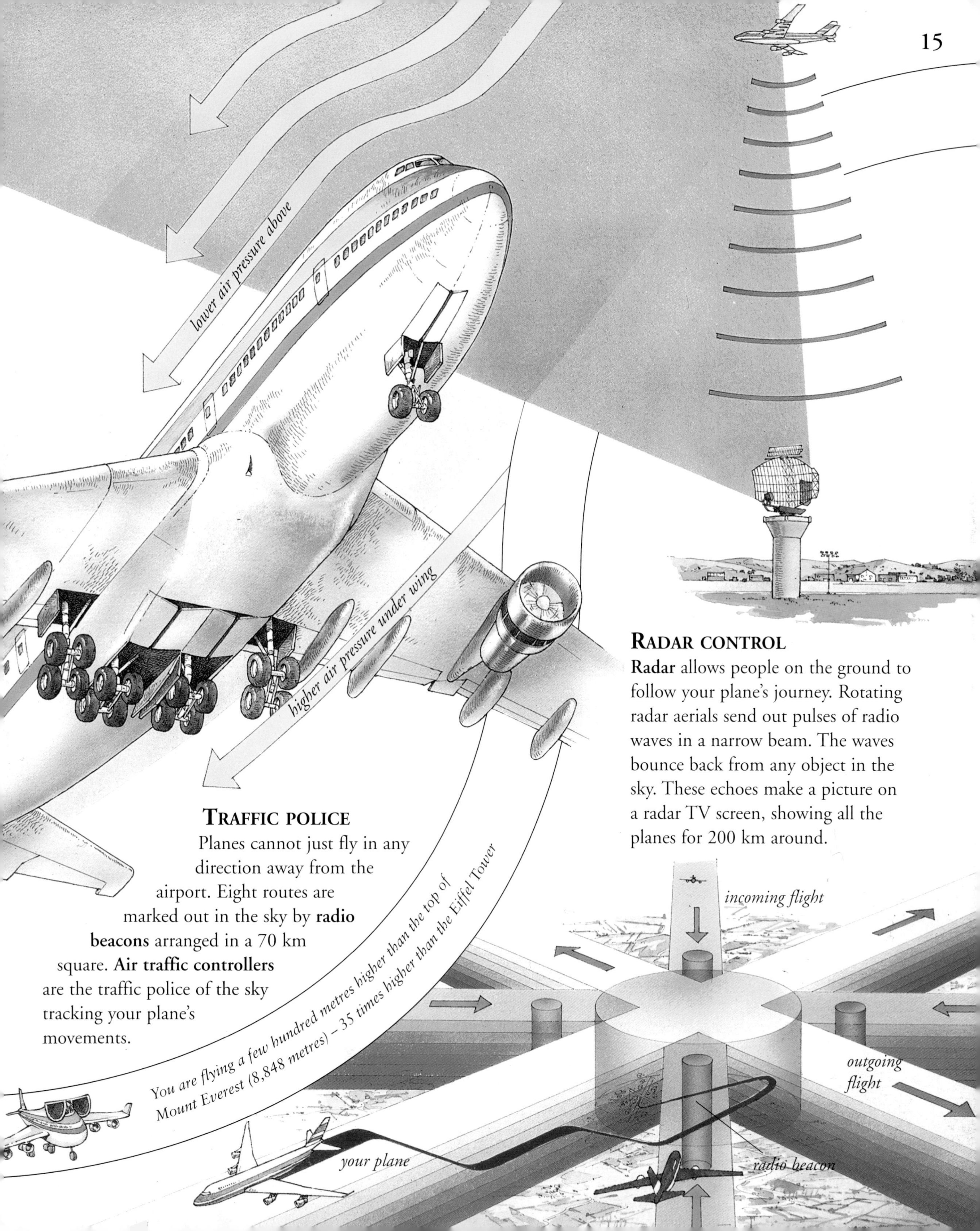

lower air pressure above

higher air pressure under wing

RADAR CONTROL

Radar allows people on the ground to follow your plane's journey. Rotating radar aerials send out pulses of radio waves in a narrow beam. The waves bounce back from any object in the sky. These echoes make a picture on a radar TV screen, showing all the planes for 200 km around.

TRAFFIC POLICE

Planes cannot just fly in any direction away from the airport. Eight routes are marked out in the sky by **radio beacons** arranged in a 70 km square. **Air traffic controllers** are the traffic police of the sky tracking your plane's movements.

You are flying a few hundred metres higher than the top of Mount Everest (8,848 metres) – 35 times higher than the Eiffel Tower

incoming flight

outgoing flight

your plane

radio beacon

air brakes

spoilers

aileron

rudder

elevator

elevator

AILERONS AND ELEVATORS

At the rear edge of each wing is a
hinged flap called an **aileron**. When
the aileron on one wing swings
down, the other swings up. The
tailplane is like a small wing at the rear
of the plane. Flaps called elevators on the
tailplane move up and down together.
The **rudder** on the tail swings from side
to side.

2.40 Dad's fountain pen has leaked all over
his shirt because of the cabin pressure

CLIMBING INTO THE SKY

You are steadily climbing away from the
airport. The plane's wings hold you up in
the air and the engines are pushing you
forwards. On the wings and tail there are
hinged flaps that can move up and down
or from side to side. These parts are
called control surfaces and they help to
steer the plane. Your plane climbs
because the control surfaces are
set to keep the tail down and
the nose pointed up
into the sky.

MOVING ON UP

You are climbing because the pilot has pulled
the control column back towards himself. This
movement has swung the elevators on the
tailplane upwards. Air rushing over the top of
the tailplane pushes against the elevators. The
result is a force that makes the tail drop.
The wings are now tilted so that the
air pushes harder against their
undersides, producing more **lift**.

*The arrows show the
exaggerated movement of
ailerons, elevators and rudder
to execute a right-hand
banked turn.*

HOW DOES A JET ENGINE WORK?

Fuel burns in the combustion chamber of the jet engine, producing searingly hot gases at high pressure. The gases roar through the blades of a power turbine as they leave the engine. The blades are angled like propellers so that the turbine spins at high speed. The power turbine drives a compressor turbine at the front of the engine which forces air into the combustion chamber. Overall, a jet engine is just a set of fans connected together.

2.5 metre fan

compressor turbine

bypass air

burning fuel

air

bypass air

power turbine (driven by hot expanding gases)

combustion chamber

TURBOFAN POWER

Each of the jet engines is as big as a family car. Passenger planes use turbofan engines which have an extra-large 2.5 metre fan at the front.

You are travelling at about one-third the speed of a rifle bullet

FOLLOWING THE CONTRAIL

Jet engines burn liquid aviation kerosene. Each tonne of this fuel uses up about three tonnes of oxygen from the air. One tonne of steam and three tonnes of carbon dioxide gas are dumped back into the air. The steam forms a white 'contrail' in the sky.

FLYING THROUGH THE AIR

On the **flight deck** at the front of the plane, the captain sits in the left-hand seat and the co-pilot sits on the right. Both are fully-qualified pilots. In front of each seat is an identical set of controls. Between them are four throttle levers that adjust the power of the engines. The captain steers a course away from the airport by moving the **control column** with his hands and the **rudder pedals** with his feet.

OPPOSING FORCES

Shut your eyes and you would hardly know you're moving. You cannot feel the plane's motion because it is held steady by two sets of opposing forces. The upward **lift** on the wings exactly balances the downward weight of the plane. Rushing air drags against the plane's skin and tries to slow it down. This force is balanced by the forward **thrust** of the engines.

Sensors detect how the plane is moving and its position in the air. They feed information to the Inertial Guidance System

lift

weight (gravity)

drag

thrust

flight control computer (input route)

control column

radio

The flight plan tells the Navigation System the route of the flight

The Inertial Guidance System tells the autopilot where it thinks the plane is

STEERING THE PLANE

The **ailerons** are found at the rear edge of each wing. They move when the pilot twists the hand grips at the top of his control column. Each aileron swings up or down in the opposite direction to the other one. The rushing air makes one wing drop while the other rises. This movement is called 'rolling'.

The **rudder** is attached to the rear of the **tailplane**. Swinging the rudder to one side pushes the tail in the opposite direction. This movement is called 'yawing'. The pilot must use rudder and ailerons together to make the plane fly in a circle.

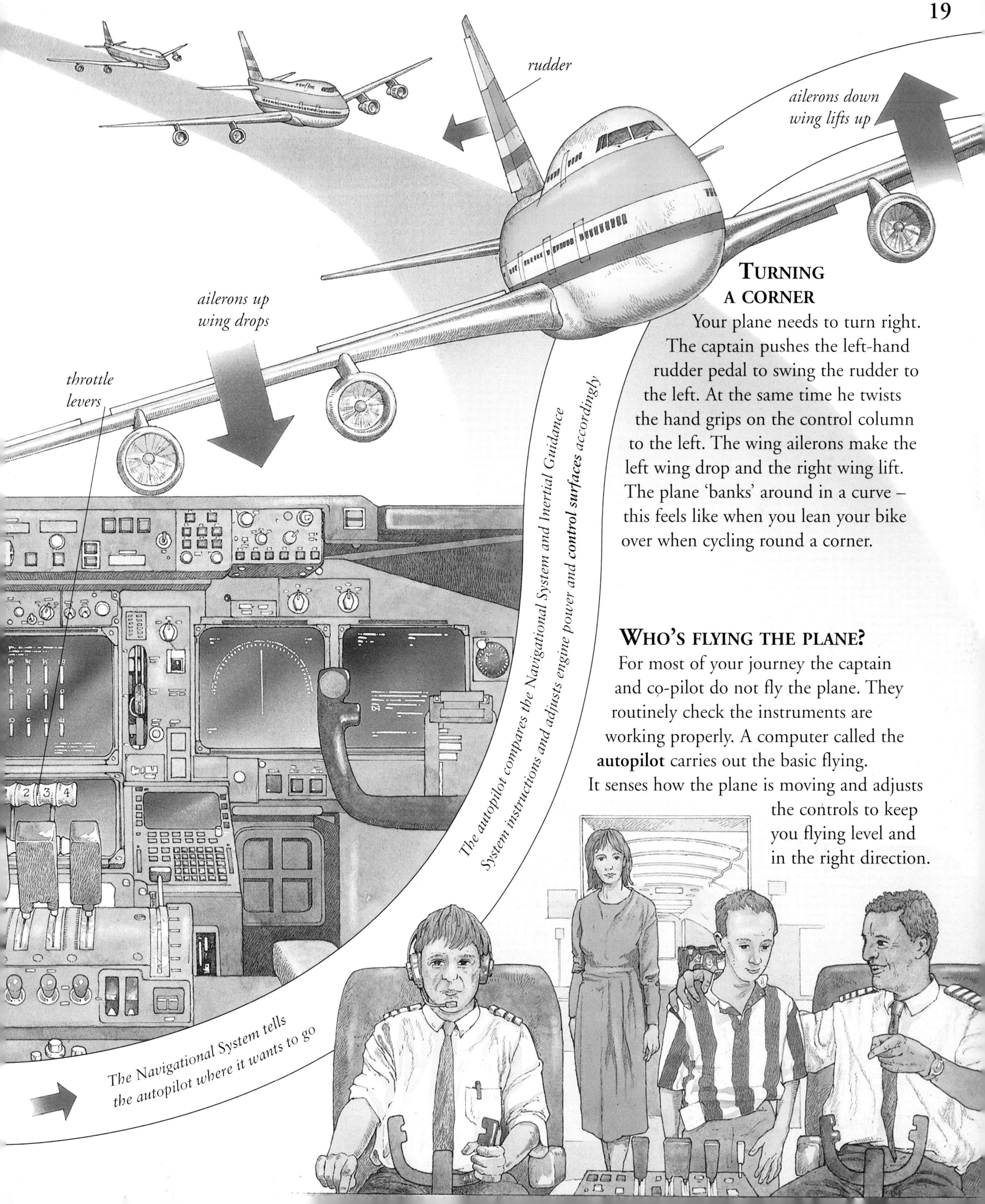

rudder

ailerons down
wing lifts up

ailerons up
wing drops

throttle
levels

The autopilot compares the Navigational System and Inertial Guidance
System instructions and adjusts engine power and control surfaces accordingly

TURNING A CORNER

Your plane needs to turn right. The captain pushes the left-hand rudder pedal to swing the rudder to the left. At the same time he twists the hand grips on the control column to the left. The wing ailerons make the left wing drop and the right wing lift. The plane 'banks' around in a curve – this feels like when you lean your bike over when cycling round a corner.

WHO'S FLYING THE PLANE?

For most of your journey the captain and co-pilot do not fly the plane. They routinely check the instruments are working properly. A computer called the **autopilot** carries out the basic flying. It senses how the plane is moving and adjusts the controls to keep you flying level and in the right direction.

The Navigational System tells the autopilot where it wants to go

*outward flight
track Alpha*

1.40 ask if you can go onto the flight deck. You hear the pilots using the following nautical terms:

SAFE ROUTES

You will fly across the Atlantic in an **air corridor** called track Alpha. It is 110 km away from the next one, track Bravo. Each track is divided into a series of flight levels stacked 600 metres above each other. Some tracks line up with the **jet stream** which is a high-**altitude** current of air blasting eastwards at 150 kph. Planes travelling from the USA to Europe will fly with the jet stream, perhaps cutting an hour off the journey.

CHECK AND DOUBLE CHECK

Over land, the pilot uses local **radio beacons** to check the plane's position. There are no beacons for checking over the sea. The pilot relies instead on the **Inertial Guidance System** (IGS).

track Alpha

flight levels

600 metres

homeward flight

Three computers calculate the plane's position by measuring the speed and direction. At regular intervals, the pilot checks that the three computers agree with each other.

HELLO AC 142...

Your pilot uses his radio to talk with **air traffic controllers** on the ground. As you fly across the ocean you are handed on from one controller to the next. The pilot must talk with both controllers during hand-over. Passengers are not allowed to use laptop computers. They transmit signals that can interfere with the **flight deck** computers guiding the plane.

WATCHING TV

Your modern 747 jumbo jet is fitted with a 'glass cockpit'. Instead of facing dozens of dials, lamps and gauges, each pilot sits in front of just two glass TV screens about 20 centimetres square.

THE GLASS COCKPIT

Below, the screen on the right gives information about the engines.

The screen in the centre shows where the plane is flying. The plane is represented by the white triangle at the bottom of the screen. The purple line shows where the route is heading and where the next turn must be made.

The left hand screen shows how the plane is flying. It gives details of altitude, speed, and direction. It also displays an **artificial horizon** which shows whether the plane is flying level.

SHOWING ON RADAR

Air traffic controllers use **radar** to locate planes as far as 200 km away. All passenger jets carry a **transponder** in their bellies. When a radar pulse from the ground bounces off the plane, the transponder adds information to the echo. A block of numbers and letters appear on the controller's screen showing your plane's identification code, **altitude**, course and speed.

Turn to starboard 10 degrees 100 nautical miles (= slight turn to the right) (= 185 km)

Turn to port 90 degrees (= turn sharp left)

Height 3-2-0 (= 32,000 feet)

Speed 540 knots (= 1,000 kph)

THE STORM

Jet airliners fly high enough to leave most clouds far below. There is one type of cloud however that can rise up to your **altitude**. It is called a cumulonimbus cloud and there is one straight ahead. Your pilot wants to avoid these storm clouds. They contain ice and hailstones, lightning and 200 kph winds that can blow straight upwards. Large hailstones can damage the jet engines if they are sucked inside. Lightning can paralyse the **radar**, radio communications and navigation systems.

Lightning often strikes airliners and can temporarily dazzle the flightdeck crew

High-altitude hailstones are often the size of golf balls – they hit the plane at 1,000 kph, and can sometimes dent wings and damage engines

The colour-coding allows the captain to spot clouds that contain dangerously large particles. The area of red indicates ice particles and hailstones within the cloud.

WEATHER RADAR

Inside the nose of your plane is the weather radar transmitter. It has sent a fan-shaped radar beam ahead and received echoes from water droplets in the storm cloud. The radar screen on the **flight deck** shows a colour-coded slice through the cloud. This one looks nasty!

slice through the wing

hot air

hot air

FREEZING RAIN

One of the great problems at 10,000 metres is freezing rain. It can coat the plane with ice in seconds. A one-centimetre thickness cuts the wing's **lift** by half. The automatic de-icer senses that ice is forming. Hot air is piped from the jet engines to keep ice away from the engine intake and the leading edges of the wing.

CHANGE OF COURSE

Several planes have already changed course and altitude to avoid the storm. All modern airliners are equipped with a Traffic Collision Alert & Avoidance System (TCAS). It is a special sort of radar that monitors the space all around the plane. TCAS warns of any plane coming closer than 8 kilometres and gives instructions on how to avoid a collision.

Electric heating coils in the plane's windscreen keep it ice-free. Warm glass is also much tougher than freezing cold glass

EVASIVE MANOEUVRES

Your captain decides to take evasive action. He speaks with the nearest air traffic control station and asks for permission to fly off his planned course. The **air traffic controllers** know about the storm and are re-routing all nearby planes. The captain feeds the new course into the **autopilot**. You start to turn in a gentle curve.

A SPOT OF TURBULENCE

'Fasten your seat belts please, ladies and gentlemen. We are in for a bumpy ride.' The flight attendants hurry round closing the overhead lockers. There are winds blowing in all directions around the storm clouds. Pilots call these winds 'turbulence' and the plane shakes up and down as it flies through them.

PASSENGER COMFORT

It is colder than Antarctica outside – minus 50°C. The air is thinner than at the top of Mount Everest where climbers have to carry breathing apparatus. The wall between you and the outside is just 19 centimetres thick – about the width of this page. However, it is very strong and you are safe. The passenger compartment is airtight. It is pumped full of air that is constantly purified by the air conditioning unit.

cut-away of this area of the plane

There is a life jacket under each seat in case the plane makes an emergency landing on water

If the cabin pressure fails, oxygen masks automatically drop down in front of each passenger

PARDON?

How's your hearing? There is about a tonne of air inside the plane. The pressure is less than at ground level so the air sealed inside your ears is trying to escape. The extra pressure can make you feel slightly deaf. Chewing, or squeezing your nose and sucking, helps the extra air to escape and returns your hearing to normal.

TIME FOR DINNER

All the food and drink comes from the 'galleys'. Powerful electric ovens quickly heat the refrigerated pre-packed meals. There are no microwave ovens because these are effectively a **radar** transmitter firing into a closed box. Total plane radar wipe-out would occur each time a meal was warmed up!

Cabin air is external air compressed by the engines

ALL IN AN HOUR

The galleys are cramped and the flight attendants must work as a team to feed all the passengers in less than an hour. Here comes your special vegetarian meal.

WHAT'S ON AT THE MOVIES?

Flying across the Atlantic can actually be quite boring. The flight lasts six hours and meals take up less than one hour. No wonder so many passengers are now snoozing. You can listen to music on a head-set that plugs into the arm of your seat. A film is shown – there are several screens so everybody has a good view.

INSIDE THE FUSELAGE

You are travelling inside the fuselage of the plane. It has a thin aluminium skin just 6 millimetres thick – about half the width of a finger nail. It is stiffened by hundreds of aluminium ribs attached to the inside. These ribs support the plastic wall panels and fittings that are around you.

APPROACH AND LANDING

You wake up to find your journey is nearly over. The plane has joined the queue for the runway. The queue is called a **holding pattern**. You are flying 100 kilometres from the airport on an oval track 15 kilometres long and 6 kilometres wide. Below you are six other planes, one above the other. When the lowest one leaves, each remaining plane flies down another 300 metres. About 25 minutes later it is your turn and you head towards the runway.

holding pattern

300 m

17.50 the plane enters the holding pattern at 4,500 m altitude

APPROACHING THE RUNWAY

There is low cloud around the airport and the pilot is assisted by the **Instrument Landing System** (ILS). ILS transmitters on the ground send up beams of radio waves. The pilot steers the plane to keep the two lines crossed in the middle of the indicator. The plane approaches the runway at exactly the right slope.

ILS radio beam

radio beam distance markers

flight path

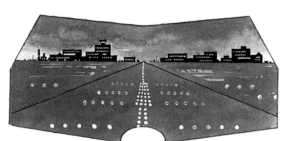

NIGHT VISION

The runway is marked out with sets of electric lamps. This picture shows how the runway appears at night when all the landing lights are lit. In case fog is too thick to land in, planes always carry enough reserve fuel to take them on to another airport.

SLOW DOWN NOW PLEASE!!!

The instant the plane lands, three things slow it down. Flaps called spoilers, or air brakes, stick up from the wings. Disc brakes attached to each wheel are screwed on. With a roar, the **thrust** of the engines is reversed to push backwards on the plane. Very soon, you are taxying slowly towards the **terminal building**.

air brakes

air brakes

disc brakes attached to wheel

flow of air

THINGS THAT GO BUMP...

Travelling at 275 kph, there is no sound from the engines as you glide onto the runway. Then with a bump and a rumble, 18 wheels slam down onto the ground. The fuel tanks are almost empty, but the plane still weighs over 250 tonnes – as heavy as 10 freight lorries.

TOUCH-DOWN

Just before touch-down, the wings look as if they are falling apart. Extra parts called flaps stick out from the front and the rear of the wings. These parts increase the area of the wings so that there is more **lift** to keep the plane flying at low speed. The plane lands at a slower speed than when it took off.

18.30 touch-down; wheel braking and engines on reverse thrust

18.23 line up with runway * 18.28 final approach at 900 m altitude

18.13 the plane leaves the bottom of the holding pattern at 1,800 m altitude

the air brakes obstruct the flow of air

DISEMBARKING

You leave the plane through the same door you entered six hours ago. A short walk brings you into the main **terminal building** but you cannot leave straight away. In all countries, officials look for people who do not have the right travel documents, smugglers and criminals. It will take another hour before you are free to enter the public part of the airport and look for your American cousins.

18.36 arrive on **stand** in front of the terminal building

IMMIGRATION

No country likes to let in people who are going to cause problems. Immigration officers check **passports** and other papers. Your family is welcome because you are tourists. You will spend lots of money and then go home again. You must have special permission to stay for a long time.

18.46 down the elevated walkway, along endless corridors and into immigration

THAT'S MY BAG!

All the baggage has been emptied from the plane while you were passing through the immigration section. It comes into the baggage hall on a **conveyor belt** and then goes round and round the baggage **carousel**. When your case goes by you drag it off the moving belt.

ANYTHING TO DECLARE?

There is a long list of things you are not allowed to bring into the USA, including illegal drugs and many sorts of animals. Customs officers check luggage and ask questions. It is just as well you decided not to bring your pet rat!

direction of earth's rotation

your route

KEEPING PEOPLE MOVING

You are just one out of 80,000 passengers who will pass through the airport today. This number is the same as the entire population of a medium-sized town in Britain. During this time, 400 aeroplanes will land and take off, load and unload. Between them they will use 40,000 tonnes of fuel – enough to fill 30 Olympic swimming pools.

19.02 find the baggage reclaim and wait for the bags;
* 19.15 get bags on trolley and in to the customs queue

19.20 there's uncle Steve waiting behind the barrier

TIME TRAVEL

Your flight took off at 12.30 and lasted for six hours – but the airport clock here says it is just 1.30 pm! You have flown against the spinning of the Earth. For you, this day will last 29 hours! Your internal body clock tells you it is half past six in the evening so you will suffer from tiredness called 'jet lag'.

THERE AT LAST!

Here are your relatives and the cab they have hired. In a few hours you will be walking through the streets of New York City. At the same time, the plane that brought you here will be taking off for Europe – cleaned, restocked, refuelled and with a fresh crew and another 400 passengers.

GLOSSARY

Aerofoil   a wing with a curved top surface and a flatter underneath surface

Aileron   a hinged **control surface** attached to the rear of each wing

Air brakes   flaps that stick straight up from a plane's wings during landing

*On landing a bird lowers its speed by tipping its wings up to face the oncoming rush of air. It uses the whole of its wings as **air brakes**.*

Air corridor   a corridor of space that each plane must fly down by itself

Air Traffic Controllers   people on the ground who monitor and direct each plane

Air tug   a squat, heavy, powerful tractor that tows planes from the aircraft **stand** to the **taxiway**

Altitude   height above the ground

Artificial horizon   a dial with a line on it that always stays horizontal no matter how the plane turns. It helps the pilot to sense where the horizon is even in the dark

Autopilot   a computer that keeps the plane flying on a pre-set course

Aviation fuel   kerosene fuel, rather like paraffin or diesel oil

Carousel   a circular **conveyor belt** on which luggage is delivered after the flight

Control column   a lever with a steering wheel, used by the pilot to control the **ailerons** and **tailplane**

Control surface   movable parts on the wings and tail used to steer the plane during flight

Conveyor belt   a wide rubber motor-driven belt on which luggage is moved

Drag   (air resistance) the force of the air against the plane's surfaces which holds it back

Flight deck   the place where the pilot and co-pilot sit; (also known as the cockpit)

Flight plan   the plane's intended route, which is given to **air traffic control** and also fed into the plane's navigational computer

Holding pattern   planes flying on an oval track while queuing to land

Inertial Guidance System (IGS) a set of sensors linked to a computer which works out the plane's location without any help from the ground

Instrument Landing System (ILS) a computer that helps to control the plane during landing

Jet stream a high-speed wind blowing far off the ground from west to east across the Atlantic

Lift an upward force on a wing, caused by air flowing around its aerofoil shape

Metal detector a machine that can sense objects made from metal

Passport a small booklet that contains a photograph and details of the traveller

Passport control the place where your passport is checked on leaving or entering a country

Push back when the **air tug** connects to the nose of the plane and pushes it off the **stand** onto the **taxiway**

Radar a device that transmits radio signals from the ground up into the air. The signals bounce off any objects in the sky, like a plane. These reflections are used to make a TV display of the plane's exact position

Radio beacon a beam of radio waves sent up from a known position on the ground. The beacon acts as a signpost for the pilot

Rudder a control surface sticking vertically upwards from the **tailplane**

Rudder pedals two pedals that the pilot uses to swing the **rudder**

Stand the parking place for a plane in front of the **terminal building**

Streamlined describes a smooth shape that slips easily through the air, with very little **drag**

Tailplane a small wing attached to the tail of a plane

Taxi to move slowly along the ground, for example from the **stand** to the runway

Taxiway a road for planes to travel from the **stand** to the runway

Terminal building the main airport building where passengers get on and off planes

Thrust the push applied to the plane by its engines

Transponder a **radar** transmitter on the plane that adds information to a radar echo returning to the ground

Undercarriage the wheels and their supports on which the plane travels along the ground

Walkie-talkie a portable battery-powered short-range radio transmitter-receiver

X-ray machine a machine used for inspecting the contents of a suitcase without opening it

X way crossroads where two taxi paths cross on the **taxiway**

INDEX

UNITS OF MEASUREMENT

SPEED	DISTANCE	VOLUME	MASS
kph = kilometres per hour (walking speed = 5 kph)	km = kilometres m = metres	1 litre = 1.8 pints = 4 cupfulls	1 tonne = 1,000 kg = 1 family car
mph = miles per hour	1,000 km = 625 miles	4.54 litres = 1 UK gallon = 1 bucketfull	
1,000 kph = 625 mph	1,000 miles = 1,600 km	3.39 litres = 1 US gallon	
1,000 mph = 1,600 kph	10,000 metres = 10 km = 6.25 miles		